TIME TO PUT YOUR FEET UP!

7 STORIES AND BISCUIT RECIPES TO RELAX WITH

by

SUE JOHNSON

This book is dedicated to anyone who needs a

mug of tea, a biscuit, a comfy chair to relax in

and a story to read.

TIME TO PUT YOUR FEET UP!
7 STORIES AND BISCUIT RECIPES
TO RELAX WITH

CONTENTS	Page

RACHEL'S BIRTHDAY

RACHEL'S BIRTHDAY

On the way to the gallery, I followed a trail of yellow sycamore leaves weaving like strange footprints along the damp pavement. I smiled, remembering how Mum would've done a silly dance or leapt from leaf to leaf. She didn't care what people thought.

"It's important to play, Rachel," she said, "however old you are."

Dad cared what people thought and he said Mum should act her age not her shoe size.

I'd forgotten that until now. It must be something about the autumn leaves, stirring the memories.

By the time I reached the gallery, I was feeling nervous again. Maybe this was the wrong thing to do and it was too late to put back the clock. I took a deep breath and pushed my way through the chrome and glass doors.

The canvases in the first room were landscapes done in oils. The colours were vibrant – yellow, pink, apricot, purple and gold. My mother couldn't have painted these pictures. They weren't the "whimsical daubings" Dad had made fun of all those years ago.

Then I saw the landscape entitled "Last Holiday" – the shimmering skyline of Venice under rain clouds. I gazed at the ice-cream colours of the buildings – pistachio, chocolate, raspberry and melon – remembering the crackling heat of the day that had ended with a thunderstorm.

I was eleven and it was the first time we'd been abroad on holiday, so everything was new and touched with a special kind of magic. That evening, we'd eaten pizzas in a little café near St Mark's Square, watching in amazement as the rain fell like big silver coins from the purple and grey sky, rapidly flooding the pathways. We'd waited in the café until the owner was ready to close, and then, laughing, we'd put on the yellow plastic macs he sold us, took off our shoes and paddled back to our hotel looking like a line of rubber ducks.

After we got home from that holiday, the rows between Mum and Dad got worse. I heard them arguing long after I'd gone to bed – mainly about her art stuff and the way she kept the house.

"If you wanted someone house-proud, Pete, you should've married your mother, not me," I heard her shout.

"I just want you to give up all this art stuff, that's all. All it does is clutter up the place."

"That's like asking me to stop breathing. You knew what I did when you first met me…"

Mum left one night in a taxi with a collection of carrier bags. I sat shivering and crying at the top of the stairs, watching as Dad made her hand over what was left of the housekeeping money and her keys. After she'd gone, he burned her clothes and a lot of her art stuff on a bonfire in the back garden and said it was just the two of us from now on. We could sort the jobs between us. We didn't need her.

Colour and laughter faded from the house with the smell of linseed oil and turps. Dad redecorated the room Mum used as a studio and it became known as the spare bedroom. It had pink flowery wallpaper and curtains and I don't remember anyone ever staying in it.

One thing I couldn't understand was that, since she left, Mum had never tried to get in touch. The last thing she said to me before she left was that she'd write to me and explain everything. She never did. There was a hurt feeling inside me that had never faded with the passing years. We'd always been so close and then it was as if she completely vanished.

Dad said that was typical of artistic types and I should forget about her, but I couldn't. She was my Mum and I still loved her deep down, whatever she'd done. The years passed and I had no idea how to get in touch with her.

Then last week someone gave me a glossy brochure advertising an art exhibition in the new gallery in town. The Christian name of the artist was the same as Mum's – Ellaline. I told myself it couldn't be her – the woman pictured in the brochure looked too young to be my mother – but curiosity got the better of me. When I saw the painting of Venice with the three yellow-clad figures, I knew.

The next canvas was called "Still Life." I recognised my old teddy called Felix, faded and missing an ear, my pink doll's house and the cherry liqueur chocolates I used to give Mum every Christmas because she loved them so much.

I remembered how I'd hugged Felix in the months after Mum left. His faded fur soaked up the tears I cried over so many things I didn't understand and that Dad wouldn't talk about.

When I was eleven, the things the kids at school said mattered. At that age, you don't want to stand out from the crowd. My Mum was the fat lady who wore weird clothes. Dad and I used to nag her to be more conservative, but she just laughed and said: "I'd rather be myself."

I feel ashamed now at how I used to go on at her to wear a black skirt and jacket like Sarah's Mum and stop showing me up by going out in faded patchwork trousers and velvet skirts from the charity shops. I was too young then to understand that's what made her special. I knew I'd hurt her feelings, but I was too bothered about what my friends said to stop.

When Dad saw her in the divorce court, he said she looked like the back end of a bus with all the colour sense of a blind chaffinch.

I thought it was odd that in all the time she'd been gone, she'd never sent me anything for my birthday or at Christmas. She was always so keen on celebrations and games of all kinds that it seemed odd. Dad said that maybe she'd changed since she left. He looked uncomfortable and his eyes didn't meet mine – which was how he always was when Mum was the topic of conversation.

He was unhappy when I decided to go to Art College when I left school.

"I suppose I can't actually stop you ruining your life, but I think you'd be better with a business studies course," he said. "You'd stand more chance of getting a proper job."

The words 'and not end up like your mother' hovered in the stale air between us.

I turned my attention to the next canvas on the gleaming white gallery wall. It was called "The Tip", which was how Dad described Mum's studio. I remembered the row they had just before she left."

"You're stifling me, Pete, don't you understand that? I need space to develop my ideas."

"What ideas are they?"

"The ones I've been trying to tell you about – my ideas for an exhibition."

"Huh, you've got about as much chance of staging an exhibition with that rubbish in the spare room as I have of flying."

"It's not a "spare room" as you put it. It's my studio."

"And what if we want someone to come and stay?"

"We never do. You never make visitors welcome."

"Why don't you get a proper job?"

"This is a proper job. You know what your problem is? You're jealous because I stand a chance of becoming successful. Jake says..."

"I wondered when his name'd crop up. You're gullible, Ellie, you know that?"

"And naïve and stupid and all those other things you usually say about me I suppose?"

The air between them seemed to crackle with electricity. The words were punctuated with bangs and thumps as Mum packed her things into an assortment of bags.

I looked at the brochure again. The woman in the picture looked slim and prosperous. The blurb said she'd won a prestigious award for her art. I felt nervous. What if she thought I'd come looking for her just to get a share of her money?

There'd been a divorce settlement years ago, which Dad said she'd fritter away on the strange people she lived with. I did wonder how he knew about the people she lived with if he claimed he didn't know her address.

I decided to head for the exit but took the wrong turning. The next section was all pictures of me – as a baby in a cute white dress edged with swansdown, in my pink ballet tutu and cuddling my pet rabbit, Rocket.

Tears were pouring down my face by now. Love shone out of every one of those canvases but I had no idea how to get in touch with her – or if she'd want me to.

Then I saw her. It had to be her, even though she'd lost a lot of weight and her hair was shorter. Nobody else could carry off that dramatic combination of deep purple and bright orange.

"Have you had your present?" she asked, as if it was seven minutes since she'd seen me and not seven years.

She led me to a tower of boxes in the next room, all wrapped in brown paper with the outer packaging torn to reveal brightly coloured birthday and Christmas paper underneath. Every package had my name and address on it. Each one had been marked 'return to sender' in Dad's handwriting.

"Why did he do it?" I asked, groping in my bag for a tissue. "Why couldn't he let me love you both?"

Mum smiled gently and her green eyes filled with tears. "Don't judge him too harshly, Rachel. He only did what he thought was right."

She searched in her squashy purple leather handbag for a tissue and dabbed her eyes. "Come on, it's time you had your present. I know it's not your birthday till tomorrow, but any time's good for a celebration."

She hadn't changed after all, I thought as I took the square brown paper wrapped package and sat next to her on the black marble bench. Ignoring the curious glances of passers-by I peeled off the outer layer of brown paper and the underlying one of shiny pink.

One of the gallery staff brought a waste bin for the paper as I carried on unwrapping. A red wine gum dropped out of the next layer. She hadn't forgotten how much I loved them – nearly as much as she adored cherry liqueur chocolates.

Half a packet of wine gums and a lot of empty wrappings later, I reached a small jewellery box. I lifted the lid to find a silver mermaid on a chain. I gave a start of surprise. How could she have known I'd planned to do a 'sea stories' theme for my final project at college? I'd done a lot of preliminary sketches of mermaids and old sailing ships, but hadn't got as far as showing them to anyone.

"How did you know I'd been thinking of mermaids?" I asked in wonder.

She winked at me. "Call it mother's intuition." She looked at her watch. "I don't know about you, but reunions always make me hungry. There's a little Italian place down the road that does brilliant lasagne and garlic bread…

As we left the gallery, the trail of yellow sycamore leaves was still there. More leaves were spiralling down from the clear blue sky.

"Catch it, Rachel, catch the leaf," said Mum as one fell towards my outstretched hands. "Now, make a wish."

I closed my eyes and made a wish that this would be the first of many fun days filling in the gaps with Mum.

"Now," she said, "walk this way."

And I followed her, hopping and skipping along the trail of leaves towards where the Italian flags fluttered outside the tiny bistro, laughing at the amused faces of passers-by. Today was a day for celebrations and silly dances along leafy pathways.

11

CHERRY & COCONUT BISCUITS

(Makes 16 biscuits)

Ingredients

60g butter
125g caster sugar
1egg
75g desiccated coconut
150g plain flour
8 glace cherries, halved

Method

Line a baking sheet with parchment. Set oven to 180C or Gas 4.

Put butter and sugar in a bowl and beat until smooth.

Add beaten egg.

Add coconut and flour.

Mix together to form a smooth, firm dough.

Divide into sixteen pieces. Roll each one into a ball. Place on the baking sheet and flatten slightly so each biscuit is about two inches in diameter. Press half a glace cherry onto the top of each one.

Bake for 15 minutes. Leave to cool on the baking tray for a few minutes and then move to a cooling rack.

FINGER PAINTING

FINGER PAINTING

The 'Copper Kettle' was crowded last Friday as Gail and I squeezed into our usual table by the window.

"How's your Mum, Sarah?" asked Gail as we ordered coffee and teacakes.

It was a question I dreaded having to answer since she and Dad split up a few months ago.

"She's gone weird," I sighed, "and I've had no help from Ben. All he keeps saying is 'good for her.' The more encouragement he gives her, the worse she gets."

I lowered my voice. "She's got dyed hair and pierced ears."

"My Mum's got a purple rinse," said Gail, "and she never goes out without wearing earrings."

I took a deep breath. "At the last count my mother had three studs in each ear and bright pink hair. She never used to be like that – she was always the sort of person who didn't stand out in a crowd. When I tried to talk to her about it the other day, she said that was why Dad left her – because she was dull and boring. Now you can't help noticing her…"

"People have their own way of coping with a marriage break-up," said Gail.

"I blame that man she met at that strange group she started going to at the Community Centre." I took a bite of my teacake and chewed fiercely. "All she talks about is Matthew. When I called for her last Tuesday morning, she was wearing a bright red t-shirt and an orange jacket because he told her they were good energy colours or some such rubbish. That's when she told me she wasn't coming to flower arranging with me any more – she was going to Matthew's yoga class instead."

I thought Gail was on my side until she phoned to say she wouldn't be meeting me at the 'Copper Kettle' this Friday.

"But we've met there every Friday since the kids started school," I said.

"Exactly," she said. "That's why I'm breaking the mould. I'm going to an art workshop with your Mum – why don't you come too?"

"So she's been getting at you as well," I said crossly. "What's she going to an art class for? She can't draw."

"They take you right back to basics – finger painting and so on." Gail sounded excited.

"I can't think of anything worse," I said, repressing a shudder. "I was glad when the kids got through that stage – all those mucky fingerprints!"

"Stay in your nice cosy rut then," Gail cooed as she hung up.

I went to see Mum. She'd taken down the familiar pale blue kitchen curtains and put up garish orange ones with gold spirals.

"I painted them myself," she said proudly, pouring us glasses of white wine instead of putting the kettle on like she used to. She opened a packet of spicy nibbles that looked guaranteed to give you indigestion. There was no sign of the cakes and biscuits she usually baked.

Mum was wearing patchwork trousers and a lime green t-shirt. Her feet were bare.

"Dad always said women should grow old gracefully," I said.

"He didn't like living with the result though, did he?" said Mum. "I gave him a shock I can tell you. He came round the other night – he's obviously not having as much fun with that bleached

16

barmaid as he expected. He wanted us to get back together." She took a sip of wine. "No way, I told him, I'm having too much fun."

"Life should be full of new experiences, Sarah," she went on, laying her silver-ringed hand on top of mine. "Matthew says being spontaneous keeps you young."

"I am spontaneous," I said huffily.

"Really?" said Mum. "Make a list of ten new things you've tried this year."

While my bath was running that night I tried to make a list, but I couldn't think of anything – apart from trying a new brand of strawberry yogurt they had on offer at the Co-op.

I looked at myself in the mirror. Mum was right. If I wasn't careful I'd end up just like she used to be – the sort of person that nobody really noticed.

I decided not to go shopping on Friday. Before I left the house I sprayed on my expensive Sunday perfume and wore the orange silk scarf Mum gave me last week that I'd pushed to the back of a drawer thinking it was too bright.

When I arrived at the Community Centre, Mum and Gail were ordering cinnamon lattes.

"I worry about Sarah," Mum was saying. "She should broaden her horizons while she's got the chance – before Ben goes off with someone more exciting."

I hesitated by the coffee bar for a few minutes before I placed my order. I'd never tried a ginger latte before. It wasn't much, but it was a start.

Mum's face lit up when she saw me. Her pink hair didn't look that bad now I'd got used to it – and she'd got nice ears, the sort that should be shown off.

As I sipped my latte, I noticed someone in the hall beyond laying out sheets of paper and trays of paint. Mum, Gail and the rest of the class raced towards the door, kicking off their shoes as they went.

"Come on, Sarah, join in." Mum was dancing in a tray of orange paint, holding out her hands to me.

I hesitated for a fraction of a second before I kicked off my sandals and stepped into the tray of sunshine yellow paint next to hers.

WHITE CHOCOLATE & CRANBERRY COOKIES

Makes 16 biscuits

<u>Ingredients</u>

90g plain flour
Half a tsp baking powder
Half a tsp bicarbonate of soda
100g butter
1 tsp vanilla essence
100g soft brown sugar
25g caster sugar
1 egg
80g porridge oats
70g white chocolate – chopped
70g dried cranberries

<u>Method</u>

Preheat the oven to 180C/Gas4. Line a baking sheet with parchment.

Sift the flour, baking powder and bicarbonate of soda in a bowl and set aside.

In another bowl, beat together the butter, vanilla and sugar.

Add the beaten egg, oats, flour mixture, chocolate and cranberries.

Divide the mixture into 16 and place on the baking sheet.

Bake for ten minutes. Allow to cool for a few minutes on the baking tray before moving to a cooling rack.

STATUES

STATUES

My friend Claire knows all there is to know about Feng shui and herbal remedies. She went on a special course to help her find her soul mate. It involved clearing a lot of clutter and making room for a man in her life. She even made space for his clothes in one of her wardrobes.

I know you're probably laughing at anyone going to those lengths to find the man of her dreams – but it worked. She met Dave on one of her trips to the charity shop clearing clutter – he held the door open for her and smiled, her heart did a somersault and they've been inseparable ever since. They're planning a spring wedding and Claire looks – smug.

Everything was going well with her life – and I was pleased for her. It just seemed that nothing was going right with mine. I'd got a job in a local museum and an end-of-terrace house with a rambling overgrown garden, and I knew I should be thankful. I was thankful, but, like Claire, I longed for the right person to share it with.

I'd tried clearing clutter and moving furniture around, but so far nothing had worked.

21

Then about ten days ago, we had a violent thunderstorm. Tiles were torn from the roof and rain poured in through my bedroom ceiling. I ended up with loads of insurance forms to fill in and the only compensation was that Rob who arrived on Monday morning to repair the damage was drop-dead gorgeous.

He had melting brown eyes and a generous smile. He was tall with broad shoulders and there was a triangular hole in his blue t-shirt just under his left shoulder blade that I longed to put my finger through and touch the brown skin underneath. I knew what Claire meant about her heart doing a somersault. The only problem was he didn't seem to feel the same about me.

When I passed him a mug of coffee that first morning, I'd felt a jolt of electricity as my fingers accidentally touched his. I was sure he must've felt it too, but his face gave nothing away.

"You'll be glad to know I'll be finished by Friday," he said when he finished work on Wednesday.

"What can I do, Claire?" I asked when she called round that evening for a glass of wine. "We get on well, but he doesn't seem interested in taking things any further."

"Maybe he's waiting for you to ask him out?" she said.

22

I shook my head. "It wouldn't feel right."

"There's a blockage here somewhere." Claire walked slowly round the garden, like a bloodhound on the scent of a criminal.

She stopped in the middle of the lawn. "It's your statue." She pointed towards the Greek goddess standing in the middle of my herb patch, the stone folds of her dress modestly draping her curvaceous figure. She had the sort of beauty and poise that I'd always wanted. I'd found her in a dingy corner of the garden centre surrounded by a group of seedy looking gnomes. One of them reminded me of the boyfriend I'd just split up with and I felt I had to take her home with me.

"Do you mean I should get rid of her?" I asked, feeling sad at the thought of it.

"You don't need to get rid of her, Sarah," said Claire. "You just need to get her a mate."

At the garden centre the next morning I found the perfect partner for her – a Greek god with rippling muscles, wearing nothing but a fig-leaf. Two men from the garden centre delivered him later that day, struggling under the weight of his athletic form.

Rob noticed the new statue when he arrived on Thursday morning.

"Making a collection of them, are you?" he asked with his usual cheeky grin, whistling as he got his tools together.

By Friday morning, nothing had changed. Rob was as friendly as ever, but he hadn't made a single move towards me.

"Soon be finished and out of your way," he said as we drank our coffee together in the garden.

He looked up at the sky. "From the look of those clouds, I'll be lucky to get finished without getting a soaking."

I thought I detected a note of regret in his voice, but his cheeky grin flashed again. "At least your roof won't leak this time."

I turned away so he wouldn't see the tears in my eyes. I couldn't bear the thought of not seeing him anymore.

I phoned Claire. "What can I do, he'll be going soon and he doesn't seem interested in me at all?"

"Getting the other statue should've worked," she said.

"Well, it hasn't," I snapped.

"Where did the men from the garden centre put the new one?"

24

"In the garden, of course," I said, feeling that this conversation wasn't getting us anywhere.

"Obviously," she said, "but are they looking at each other?"

"Well…no. He's got his back to her."

"I despair of you sometimes, Sarah," she said. "What do you expect?"

"I'll call you back later," I said, noticing that Rob was hovering.

"All finished," he said, clearing away the last of his tools, "and the rain's just starting."

My hand shook as I wrote him a cheque, knowing that whatever I did with the statues now, it was too late because in a few minutes he'd be gone from my life.

I couldn't bear to see him drive away, so I went out into the garden. The first big splashes of rain had changed the colour of the statues from dove grey to charcoal. Thunder rumbled and the sky was an eerie yellow patterned with bruised-plum coloured clouds.

Despite knowing it was too late, I tried to turn the male statue so he was facing the Greek lady. He was far too heavy for me and I lost my grip on the damp stone. The statue fell headlong into a clump of sapphire coloured lobelia and I ended up in a crumpled heap on the rain-slicked ground, my left ankle throbbing with pain.

A few minutes later, I heard the splutter of tyres on gravel, the slam of a car door and then Rob was racing down the garden towards me.

"Sarah," he said. "I came back because I had a feeling there was something wrong."

He helped me to my feet and carried me into the cottage, the warmth of his body reaching me through his damp t-shirt. I could feel the thudding of his heart next to mine.

He settled me on the sofa, bandaged my ankle carefully and made me a mug of hot sweet tea.

"I don't like to leave you like this," he said sitting down next to me. "You might go into shock."

I didn't like to say I already had – being held close by him when I'd thought that all was lost had done weird things to my heartbeat.

"Please don't go." I hadn't meant to say that – the words just came out.

Rob lifted my chin with a rough forefinger and gazed into my eyes. "You've no idea how hard it's been to keep my hands off you this week – but I've got this old fashioned rule that I don't mix business and pleasure."

He smiled. "But since I'm not working for you any more…"

He leaned towards me and our lips met in a passionate kiss that made me feel as if I'd just had a ride on a fairground roller-coaster.

From the look on his face, it was clear that Rob felt the same.

Later, after the rain had stopped, we went out into the garden to look at the stars. There was a path of silver moonlight across the garden and a feeling of magic in the warm air.

I noticed that Rob had moved the statues so they were standing face to face, their stone feet surrounded by blue lobelia and orange nasturtiums. It was probably my imagination, but they looked happy too.

PEANUT BUTTER COOKIES

Makes 16 biscuits

<u>Ingredients</u>

45g smooth peanut butter
50g butter
50g caster sugar
45g light brown sugar
1 egg
100g plain flour
1 tsp baking powder
Grated zest from half an orange
50g chopped unsalted peanuts

<u>Method</u>

Preheat the oven to 180C/Gas 4. Line a baking sheet with parchment.

Cream the peanut butter, butter and sugar.

Add the egg.

Add flour, orange zest, baking powder and peanuts.

Divide the mixture into sixteen pieces. Roll each one into a ball. Place on the baking sheet and flatten each one slightly with the back of a fork.

Bake for 20 minutes.

Allow to cool for a few minutes after removing from the oven and then move the biscuits to a wire cooling rack.

WILLIAM'S PARROT

WILLIAM'S PARROT

I watched Tom walk down the path, wishing he hadn't left me to deal with Mr Jenkins this afternoon. I had a feeling that, as usual, we'd come off worse.

We'd first met Mr Jenkins when Tom's Gran died and we needed to sell some of her furniture. I hadn't liked him from the start – he had a face the colour of raw steak and a shifty expression in his bloodshot dark eyes

Tom and I knew nothing about antiques and so at first we believed everything Mr Jenkins told us. Then a coal-scuttle of Gran's that Mr Jenkins offered to dispose of for us ended up as the 'star buy of the week' in his shop in Pendlebury.

We wouldn't have known about the coal-scuttle if my friend Lucy hadn't gone into the shop and asked about it. Mr Jenkins had told her where he got it from, and how he instantly spotted how valuable it was. He'd told us it was worthless.

"Probably cost me money to have it taken away," were his exact words.

"I wouldn't have anything else to do with him, Claire," said Lucy. "It makes me wonder if he gave you a fair price for everything else."

I was quite sure he hadn't but Tom was far more trusting than me.

"It was our fault for not doing a bit more research before we called him in," he said. "We should've had more idea of what we were getting rid of and set a minimum price. I've learned a lot from looking on the internet."

We'd spent ages discussing how we could improve our financial situation. We didn't really want to sell any more of Gran's furniture, but money had been tight since William was born. He was three now and at Playgroup and had grown so much that he needed a new bed. Then, a few days ago the boiler blew up and even our clever plumber was unable to help.

Tom had spent yesterday lunchtime on the internet in the library, finding out more about the sideboard that Gran had left us.

"It's made of rosewood and therefore quite valuable," he said, his blue eyes lighting up with excitement. "I saw a picture of one just like ours and it was valued at £1000. Just think, Claire – all our financial problems solved in one go."

I didn't really want to sell the sideboard - I'd grown rather attached to it. It was a useful place to keep the plates and cutlery and I loved the soft gleam of the wood when it was polished.

"Mr Jenkins' eyes will pop out of his head when he sees this," said Tom when he showed me the pictures he'd printed off the computer in the library. "Make sure you don't let it go for less than £750. You know what he's like – he won't pay more than he has to."

"What do you mean? You don't expect me to deal with him, do you?" I stared at Tom in horror across the breakfast table. "Can't you come home and deal with him?"

"Sorry, I've got a meeting this afternoon. You'll charm the money out of him, Claire, no problem," said Tom. "I've every confidence in you."

I wished I could believe him. My stomach churned at the thought of facing Mr Jenkins on my own.

Thankfully, I had other things to occupy my mind before he was due to arrive at two o'clock. I had to get William up and dressed and into Playgroup for nine o'clock. Then I had a cleaning job to do at the local Arts Centre before I picked him up again at twelve.

Adding to my ever-present worries about money – or the lack of it - was, what could I buy Tom for his birthday next week? He'd said not to bother because money was tight, but I knew I had to get him something. Maybe if Mr Jenkins coughed up as much as Tom hoped he would, then there would be a little bit left over to buy him something nice.

William had been painting at Playgroup that morning. When I arrived to pick him up, he was grinning from ear to ear and had splashes of red paint in his hair and a dab on his cheek.

"Ben kept getting in the way," he said as he led the way to the kitchen and proudly showed me the painting he'd done, hanging up to dry on the indoor washing line.

"Sorry, we forgot to put his name on it," said one of the helpers. "But he knows which is his anyway. It's very – distinctive," she added.

The painting was a vibrant mixture of red, green and yellow with a strange black squiggle at the bottom of the page. The paint was dry, so I carried it carefully in one hand, holding William's hand firmly in the other.

"What's the painting about?" I asked as we walked home for hot chocolate and toasted cheese. I'd been on one of those Playgroup training days where we'd been told not to ask 'what is it?' but to let the child talk about their picture.

William looked up at me with wide blue eyes. "It's a parrot," he said. "And he lives in the jungle. And that there – he pointed to the bottom of the page – that's a worm he's just going to eat."

I wasn't sure if parrots ate worms but I didn't say anything.

"Perhaps we could give it to Daddy for his birthday," I said. "When we've had our lunch, I'll see if I can find a frame for it."

William was more interested in the lunchtime programmes on the telly and the invitation to a birthday party he'd been given.

While he was having a nap, I rummaged in the loft and found a wooden frame and a pale yellow mount that echoed the colour of what I assumed was the parrot's beak. The frame was a bit old-fashioned but it was the best I could do and I knew Tom would love the painting anyway.

34

Until I went into the dining room for a duster to give the frame a final polish and caught sight of the rosewood sideboard, I'd forgotten that Mr Jenkins was calling at two o'clock. My heart sank when I saw his white van pull up outside.

I hastily put William's picture on the table in the hall while I went to open the front door.

Mr Jenkins walked in, exuding the combined smells of stale sweat and Brut after-shave. He looked critically at the sideboard from every possible angle, opened drawers and looked inside, sucked his teeth and finally shook his head.

"If it had been proper rosewood, I'd have snapped it up," he said. "But it isn't. It's a cheap imitation, very popular in the late nineteenth century. To be honest with you, Mrs Mitchell, I'm over-run with stuff like this. I'll do you a favour and take it away for twenty quid, but I can't offer you any more than that…"

I felt as if I'd just had a bucket of icy water thrown over me. I didn't know what I was going to say to Tom when he came home. There was no way I'd give the sideboard away for a ridiculous amount like twenty pounds, but the fact remained we needed the money and my head span dizzily wondering where we'd find it.

35

Feeling numb, I moved towards the front door to let Mr

Jenkins out. He looked cross because he'd had a wasted journey.

His face changed when he caught sight of William's picture.

"Now this is interesting." He picked it up and studied it

closely. "Where have you been hiding this, Mrs Mitchell?"

He got a magnifying glass out of his pocket and scanned

William's parrot carefully, his face going even redder with

excitement.

"If I'm not mistaken, that's an early Cameron Pritchard – see

the signature at the bottom. Often called the wriggly worm."

"That's because it is a wriggly worm," I only just stopped

myself saying.

He babbled on excitedly. "There was one of these on

Antiques Roadshow the other week. Look – let's not beat around the

bush. I want this painting and I'm prepared to take it now. What do

you say to £1000?

I took the money from him and handed over the painting.

William could do another picture at Playgroup tomorrow. It may not

resemble a masterpiece but I knew Tom would love it.

GINGER BISCUITS

Makes 12 biscuits

<u>Ingredients</u>

125g butter
125g soft brown sugar
1 egg yolk
1 tbsp golden syrup
180g self-raising flour
1 tsp ground ginger

<u>Method</u>

Preheat oven to 180C/Gas 4 and line a baking sheet with parchment.

Cream butter and sugar.

Add egg yolk and syrup and mix well.

Combine ginger and flour in another bowl. Sieve into the butter mixture and fold in gently.

Divide the mixture into twelve pieces and roll into balls. Place them on the baking sheet and flatten them slightly with the back of a spoon.

Bake for 15 minutes or until golden brown.

Allow to cool slightly after removing from the oven and then move the biscuits to a wire cooling rack.

WORDS IN TREES

WORDS IN TREES

My neighbour, Maureen, had an accident yesterday. Her son, Wayne, knocked on the door at eight o'clock this morning to tell me they'd kept her in hospital overnight.

I hadn't spoken to Wayne since he'd come round a few months ago to grumble about my eucalyptus tree.

"Mum doesn't like it because it blocks the light in her conservatory," he said, blinking at me with pale-lashed eyes.

"The tree was there long before your conservatory," I said.

"Does that mean you're not going to have the tree cut down?"

"Got it in one," I said, closing the door firmly on him.

Now Wayne was here again, his furtive glance flickering along the hall towards the kitchen where I'd just got a cake out of the oven. Any minute now he'd start dropping hints about needing a mug of tea to get over the shock of his mother's accident.

I'd made a vow never to let anyone from that family over my doorstep again. You see, I'd fallen for that one when I first moved here and invited Maureen in for a coffee. Within a few hours it was all round Compton Close that I'd got loads of silver ornaments and original paintings. With a foghorn voice like Maureen's it could've alerted every burglar for miles around.

"I don't understand how it happened," Wayne said, his slippery gaze flickering across my face and back along the hall. "She fell out of the bedroom window onto the conservatory roof. It's not like she's old or gets giddy turns…"

I shut my eyes, imagining Maureen with her dyed marmalade coloured hair and fingernails to match sailing through the air. The drama of being taken away in an ambulance would give her celebrity status for at least a week. Knowing her, she'd probably already contacted the local papers.

"She was lucky she didn't go through the glass," Wayne said. "I'm surprised you never heard anything. There was a terrific bang when she fell and if I hadn't been there she'd have spent all night on the conservatory roof."

"I'd forgotten you were home for a while," I said.

I should've remembered that Wayne never stayed in any job for more than a few weeks. No sooner was Maureen crowing about the fantastic job Wayne had just landed, than he was back and staying with her again, complaining bitterly about the unfair treatment he'd had from yet another employer.

It was lucky she didn't go through the roof. It's all cracked and a man's just come and said it's unsafe and needs to be taken down. It was a good job I was here to help her back in."

I coughed to hide the laughter bubbling up inside me at the thought of Maureen having to spend the night on the conservatory roof. There'd be a lot to see from up there. And a lot to talk about afterwards – enough to guarantee her plenty of invitations to afternoon tea.

I'm sure Maureen only wanted my eucalyptus tree cut down because it blocked her view of the new patio I'd had put in and she wanted to see who came to visit me.

She used to spend half the day cleaning the inside of her conservatory, standing on steps so she could reach the glass panels at the top of the wall that were decorated with showy red and blue flowers. She'd stand there for ages, squinting through the clear glass gaps, trying to spot the changes I'd made to the garden.

When I put in my herb garden she was convinced I was growing illegal substances. She gossiped about it so much that I ended up with a visit from the local community policeman. Somebody – Maureen denied it was her – had tipped them off that I needed checking up on.

Wayne was still standing on my doorstep looking at me furtively like a rat peeping out of a hole in the wall. "Are you sure you never heard anything?"

I shook my head. I didn't trust myself to speak because the laughter was bubbling up again.

"My toy-boy stayed the night – I'd probably got my head under the duvet."

Wayne goggled at me and I could tell he was storing the information up to tell Maureen when he visited her in hospital.

"Only joking," I said. "Your Mum always says I'm a first class fibber."

Wayne flushed scarlet.

"She didn't mean it like that… It was just…"

"Don't worry about it," I said waving my hand airily. "My teacher at junior school always said I was a first class storyteller."

Mind you, I'd have thought Maureen would've learned her lesson by now and not taken any notice of anything I said.

There was the time when my friend John called on his way to a business meeting. Maureen – leaning out of her front window this time – put two and two together and decided he was an estate agent and that I was selling up and moving. She was so convinced she told everybody in the Close.

One of the neighbours asked me when I was moving. I decided to have some fun and spread some gossip of my own.

"Oh no, that wasn't an estate agent, that was my gynaecologist," I said, sticking my middle-aged stomach out. "You've no idea what I have to pay him to do a home visit."

I must have been a convincing liar because I received two pairs of bootees and a matinee jacket from her and another neighbour sent her daughter, Kelly, round asking if she could babysit for me in the future.

"Someone seems to have got the wrong end of the stick. What makes you think I'm having a baby? I'm far too old for that sort of thing."

Kelly's plump face flushed a delicate shade of beetroot. "But someone said you had a home visit from a gyny-something…"

"And so I did," I said, crossing my fingers behind my back. "And I think someone may have jumped to the wrong conclusions. It doesn't do to believe all you hear, Kelly."

After she'd gone, I'd had a chuckle to myself, thinking that Maureen would be mad that I'd got the better of her again. I just wished she'd leave me alone and stop her disruptive gossiping.

I decided to let the eucalyptus tree grow after she complained to the Council about the beehive I'd found in a junk shop. As soon as I saw it lying dusty and neglected in a corner of the shop, it reminded me of my grandfather and how I used to like watching him from a safe distance when he looked after his bees. Even though I had no intention of keeping bees myself, I decided to repaint the hive and have it as a garden ornament.

Within hours of me positioning the beehive in my herbaceous border, Maureen had started work on a petition to stop me keeping dangerous insects and had contacted the Council again. A lady came to see me and left with a smile on her face and showering me with profuse apologies, saying that she'd obviously been misinformed. I thought Maureen would've learned her lesson by then but she hadn't. She was so anxious not to miss the next instalment of my life that she even had her bedroom window replaced with one that opened wider so she could lean out and see further down my garden.

"So you've no idea how the accident happened then?" Wayne's whining voice dragged me back to the present.

"No idea at all," I said. "It's a complete mystery. Sorry I can't ask you in. I'm busy right now."

He'd turned away and shambled back towards Maureen's house and I closed the door feeling relieved to have got rid of him.

I sat in the sitting room relaxing with a mug of tea, smiling as I went over the events of the last few months in my mind. I knew exactly how Maureen's accident had happened – and so did she, except that she probably wouldn't want to admit the truth to her friends. Hopefully, from now on she'd leave me alone.

I finished my tea and then got the shredder out, feeding the small pieces of white card into it. Until yesterday they were hanging in my eucalyptus tree.

Typed in very small black letters on each piece of card was the message: "if you can read this, you're leaning too far out of the window."

LEMON SHORTBREAD

Makes 16 biscuits

Ingredients

200g butter
100g caster sugar
Grated zest of one lemon
300g plain flour

Method

Preheat the oven to 160C/Gas 3 and line a baking sheet with parchment or non-stick paper.

Mix butter and sugar in a bowl. Add the lemon zest.

Then mix in the flour. Work the dough together with your hands until it forms a ball.

Roll it out to about 5mm thick. Cut out shapes with a biscuit cutter. Place on the baking sheet.

Chill in the fridge for 15 minutes before baking.

Sprinkle each biscuit with a pinch of granulated sugar and bake for 15 – 20 minutes or until pale golden brown.

Allow to cool on the tray for a few minutes before moving to a cooling rack.

CRIMSON SILK

CRIMSON SILK

Helena stood on the doorstep watching Darren walk away, the heavy rain soaking his baggy red cotton trousers.

His words scratched at her mind like a scouring pad. She didn't want to believe them. "Charlie never told anyone the truth, Helena. You're far more talented than he ever was."

Helena watched as Darren reached the corner of the road. She remembered how she hadn't wanted a male lodger in the first place, but Darren was the only person to respond to the advertisement and she needed the money. He had blue eyes that reminded her of a Mediterranean sea on a summer's day and a smile that could've melted her heart if she'd allowed it to. He wore a strange assortment of clothes – patchwork cotton trousers and a pink and orange jacket with a logo that said 'I Love Life.' Helena wondered what he did for a living.

She knew that, to him, she looked plain and uninteresting in her black dress with her hair tied back from her face but she didn't care.

It was only after she'd offered him the room that he told her he was an art teacher at the local college – the place where her beloved Charlie had taught for most of his life.

She'd almost withdrawn the offer when he'd said that. Only the thought of being able to cover her bills kept her from dwelling on the thought of someone else working in Charlie's studio and teaching the students that would have been his.

Darren looked at Helena curiously when she said there was to be no painting in her house – she couldn't bear the smell of linseed oil and turps.

"But you're an artist," he said, bewilderment clouding his blue eyes.

"Was," said Helena sharply, "a long time ago." She wondered who had been gossiping about her.

She'd come home the next day to a still life of oranges, apples and grapes placed on the sunlit kitchen table.

"Look at the way the light catches them. Doesn't it make you want to paint them?" said Darren

Helena couldn't answer him. She walked out of the kitchen and went to her bedroom, slamming the door. A short time later, she heard him rummaging in the fridge, rattling saucepans and then the insidious smell of garlic and frying meat drifted up the stairs. Since Charlie died, Helena had lost her appetite, existing on safe foods like jacket potatoes, toast and scrambled eggs – food that didn't hold memories of candlelit restaurants and loving embraces.

She sat on her bed remembering her first day at college five years ago when she walked into the lecture room and saw Charlie for the first time. She'd just finished her first exhibition of paintings, had sold a number of them and was nervously clutching a portfolio of her work.

Charlie wore blue jeans and a paint-stained black t-shirt. He was working on a green and blue landscape. The hairs on his arms glinted copper in the sun and Helena longed to touch them. He'd looked up and smiled at her, his green eyes crinkling at the corners.

After the first lecture, he invited her for lunch impressing on her that she must keep it a secret from the other students. They ate in a small French bistro a few miles away and spent the afternoon in bed in a shabby hotel.

"You've got a long way to go with your painting," Charlie said as he ran his fingers over her naked body. "I think we can call your exhibition success 'beginner's luck' – but a girl as beautiful as you doesn't need a career."

Within three months he'd proposed. Helena's parents were upset about her artistic career ending before it had begun.

"They've predicted a great future for you, darling," her mother said. "Don't throw it away. After all, Charlie's so much older than you…"

Helena had walked away before her mother could finish what she was saying. She loved and trusted Charlie. After all, he'd tried and failed to make it as an artist, so what chance did she have?

They'd married and Helena gave up her artistic career to cook and clean for Charlie. She told people she was too busy to bother about painting. Then, three years after the wedding, Charlie died of a heart attack at work.

After the funeral, Helena cleared all Charlie's paintings out of the house and painted the walls the colour of bleached bones. She couldn't think of colour without remembering Charlie and feeling sad. It was safer to live without it.

Now Darren had wheedled his way into her house, threatening to change everything.

This morning, she'd awoken to the sound of him moving furniture. Helena put on her dressing gown and went to investigate.

Darren's bedroom door stood wide open and the walls vibrated with colour – hot pink, acid green, indigo and purple. Helena recognised the paintings she'd created before she met Charlie.

"Where did you get these?"

"I found them at the back of a cupboard in my art room at the college," said Darren. "One of the other lecturers told me that Charlie had hidden them away there – just like he kept you a prisoner in this house. Why did you give up painting when you have so much potential? Why did you take any notice of someone like Charlie Phillips who never stopped cheating on you?"

Helena felt her legs go wobbly as the memories came flooding back. Charlie had sworn he'd been true to her but there had always been rumours. He'd dismissed them as people being jealous. There had always been a ready excuse for his jacket smelling of another woman's perfume – a student who'd been upset or being accidentally sprayed with scent when he was buying Helena a present. He was always buying her presents…

"You've got talent, Helena," said Darren gently, "and Charlie knew it. That's why he was jealous of you. That's why he stopped your career before it started." He touched her shoulder to bring her round to face him.

"Get out. You don't know what you're talking about." Helena backed out of the door and picked up a glass paperweight from the table on the landing.

"Charlie only cared about himself. When did he ever sell a painting? Don't let your talent go to waste Helena."

"Get out!"

"It's raining."

"I don't care."

After Darren had gone, Helena went back upstairs and stood in his bedroom staring at her forgotten paintings. Things people had said spiralled round in her head. She remembered Charlie's refusal to introduce her to his friends and how he cancelled her stand at an art exhibition before they got married because he said she wasn't ready. She remembered Charlie's sarcasm when someone referred to her as 'the talented half of the partnership.' She thought the person was just being nice – but what if it was true?

Helena looked at her painting called 'Golden Dawn' – a passionate abstract streaked with pink, apricot and gold. Tears filled her eyes as she realised how she'd missed the feel of a brush in her hand and the smell of oil paint. Darren was right – it was time she moved on.

She searched her wardrobe for the crimson silk dress she'd bought the Christmas after her wedding but never wore because Charlie went to the college party alone, saying she'd find it all very boring. He'd come home late with an excuse about staying to help clear up and accused her of being neurotic when she'd noticed lipstick on his shirt.

For the first time since he'd died, Helena felt a sense of freedom. She smoothed the soft crimson fabric over her body, admiring the way it clung to her curves. She hoped Darren would forgive her for sending him out in the rain and that they could make a fresh start. She prepared his favourite lasagne for lunch and uncorked some red wine before she rang the college asking him to come home urgently. As she waited, she felt a warm glow inside as soft as oil paint spreading across canvas as she imagined what would happen next.

CHOCOLATE CHIP COOKIES

Makes 25 biscuits

Ingredients

150g butter
80g soft brown sugar
80g granulated sugar
2 tsp vanilla extract
1 egg
225g plain flour
Half a teaspoon bicarbonate of soda
200g plain chocolate chips or chunks

Method

Preheat the oven to 180C/Gas4 and line two baking trays with parchment or lining paper.

Put butter and sugar into a bowl and beat until creamy. Add the egg and vanilla.

Sieve in the flour and bicarbonate of soda. Mix with a wooden spoon.

Add the chocolate chips.

Using a teaspoon, place small mounds of mixture on the baking tray.

Bake for 10 minutes or until light brown at the edges and slightly soft in the middle.

Leave to cool for a few minutes before transferring to a wire cooling rack.

THE GLASS ANGEL

THE GLASS ANGEL

I never thought an angel could change my life. That was until I met one on that special Saturday in September. Let me tell you what happened.

I'd taken ages to do the shopping because of meeting the angel. Mum put on her 'nobody cares about me' look when I got home. Her bottom lip stuck out like a shelf.

"I wondered when you'd be back, Ruth."

I felt like a sixteen year old again and I reminded myself that this was my house. It was one o'clock on a Saturday lunch-time, not three o'clock in the morning. Mum didn't have to stay here if she didn't like it. She had a flat that she shared with Auntie Nora and I'd been wishing for the last two years that she'd go back there.

"Nora argues all the time," Mum said. "Besides, you need watching."

Watching was the last thing I needed, especially now I might have a new man in my life. It wouldn't be long before Mum picked up on that one and sabotaged anything before it started. She always said it was for my own good. I obviously didn't have 'the knack' with men, seeing that Ben went off with the barmaid from the 'Three Kings' two months after we got engaged.

That was two years ago. Mum moved in after a row with Auntie Nora and she'd been with me ever since, moaning about my furnishings, my food and the scratching noise in the attic.

I noticed that she'd moved the chairs again. She'd taken down the abstract painting I'd put on the wall and replaced it with a little boy in Victorian clothes with tears in his eyes. Until now, I'd have tried to ignore those things – it wasn't worth causing a fuss. Today, a different voice in my head said: '*Stand up to her – don't let her push you around.*'

I smiled to myself. That'll be the angel, I thought as I carried my bags into the kitchen.

Mum followed, limping slightly. Her bad leg always got worse when she felt someone was getting at her.

"I had to take that picture down," she said. "Them colours was giving me a headache. What've you got there? Didn't you get my tablets? What's this stuff? Garlic bread? I thought I told you to get some cheap bread from that bakers up Port Street."

"Things are changing," I whispered as I unwrapped the angel.

She was made of purple stained glass, edged in silver. I stood her in the kitchen window. The light radiating from her filled the room.

I remembered what the man in the shop – David – said.

"They change your life. Some surprising things have happened to me since I started making Hannah and her sisters. Now they've led me to this gallery. And you."

He looked into my eyes when he said it. If it had been any other man I'd have said he was flattering me so I'd buy something. David was different.

Mum was still moaning about the bread.

"I can't eat that garlic bread. It gives me wind."

"Mum, why don't you go to the 'Three Kings' with Josie-next-door? She keeps asking you. They do a very good pensioners lunch on a Saturday."

"I can't leave you, can I? Lord knows what you'll be up to next. Wasting your money on heaven knows what."

I swallowed my irritation.

Mum ate the garlic bread and the Mexican bean soup I'd bought to go with it. I smiled as I thought about David's gallery and how I never intended to go in there – until I saw the angel in the window.

It was the sort of shop Mum would dismiss as 'too posh' and 'you might break something.'

Once I was inside, I was fascinated by the patterns of light on glass. The vibrant colours spoke to me and made me feel that life could get better.

"It's never too late to change," said David, as if he read my mind.

He had green eyes that reminded me of a summer sea and long hair in a ponytail – the sort of man Mum would dismiss as 'arty and unreliable' before she even got to know him.

David and I talked and laughed a lot. I spent nearly two hours with him sipping coffee and looking at his collection of rainbow-coloured angels.

It was magical. I could almost hear the whisper of small voices saying: *"Nothing will change unless you make it."*

Mum didn't like the angel.

"The money you spent on that thing would've bought me a pair of shoes."

"You've got dozens of pairs in your wardrobe."

"You know what I'm like about things with wings."

I knew all about Mum's phobia about things with wings. She couldn't stand birds, butterflies or moths. She said it made her go 'all peculiar' if there was anything like that within fifty yards of her.

"You'll have to get used to them if you're going to heaven," I said.

There was no denying I felt different. I wasn't going to let her grumpiness get me down any more.

For the first time in ages, I didn't spend all weekend doing housework. On Sunday after the rain cleared, I sat in the garden watching the diamond raindrops on the grass, looking at the pattern of light on the spiders' webs. I thought of how I always wanted to learn to paint and how Mum never encouraged that sort of thing. Now I was determined to try it.

Mum looked hostile on Monday evening when I told her I was off to join an art class.

"I'm not feeling well," she said. "I need you here to look after me."

"Josie-next-door's going to look in," I said brightly. "So you won't be on your own."

A few days later I sorted out my clothes. I took the old-fashioned skirts and jumpers Mum liked me to wear to the charity shop. I swapped them for figure-hugging jeans and silk shirts in all the colours of the rainbow. I bought expensive perfume and bubble bath.

"People will get the wrong idea about you," grumbled Mum.

"They can think what they like," I said as I went out to meet David for a drink.

As I left the house I glanced at the angel and I was sure she was smiling at me.

David said he could see the angel was doing me good. I wanted to tell him it wasn't just the angel.

"The light's coming back into your life," he said as he kissed me goodnight.

"It is. It certainly is," I said as I kissed him back.

After that I started on the house. I bought velvet cushions in jewel colours – dark blue, red, acid yellow. I bought fresh flowers, candles and pot pourri.

Mum didn't like it.

"The smell of that stuff gets on my chest. You'll have to get rid of it."

I took no notice. Things had changed.

"And another thing, Ruth. You'll need to get the man from the council in. We've got mice. I can hear them scurrying in the attic. It's not surprising with all that fancy stuff you keep buying."

I lay awake listening that night. It didn't sound like scurrying feet. It sounded to me like the soft movement of angels' wings.

When I got home from work today, Mum was packing her bags. She'd had the man from the Council round about the mice. Except it wasn't mice. We'd got bats in our attic and they had to stay there.

"There's a preservation order on them. So we can't do nothing. And you know me with anything with wings. Makes me feel bad. I knew that angel would bring bad luck but you wouldn't listen."

I watched as she zipped up the last suitcase.

"I've got a taxi to take me to Nora's. She hasn't got room for both of us. I don't know how you'll manage without me."

I helped her carry her bags downstairs.

Inside my head I was planning the special meal I'd cook for David tonight. My imagination felt like it had wings. I was planning how I'd convert the spare room into an art studio. I'd have stained glass windows and get David to make more angels for me.

I hoped that by the time Mum had the next argument with Auntie Nora, there would be even more changes in my life and there wouldn't be room for her to come and live here again.

As I waved her off in the taxi I thought I heard the flutter of wings behind me and the bubbling laughter of an angel.

OAT & RAISIN COOKIES

Makes 12 biscuits

Ingredients

50g butter
50g caster sugar
1 tbsp set honey
1 egg
1 tsp cinnamon powder
50g wholemeal flour
1 tsp baking powder
80g porridge oats
80g raisings

Method

Heat oven to 180C/Gas 4. Line a baking sheet with parchment or lining paper.

Mix together butter, sugar and honey.

Add egg and cinnamon.

In another bowl mix together flour, oats, raisins and baking powder.

Add to butter mixture.

Divide mixture into twelve equal pieces and place on baking sheet.

Bake for 10 – 12 minutes.

Remove from oven. They should be slightly soft to the touch.

Leave to cool for a few minutes and then move to a wire cooling rack.

Printed in Great Britain
by Amazon.co.uk, Ltd.,
Marston Gate.